I0766597

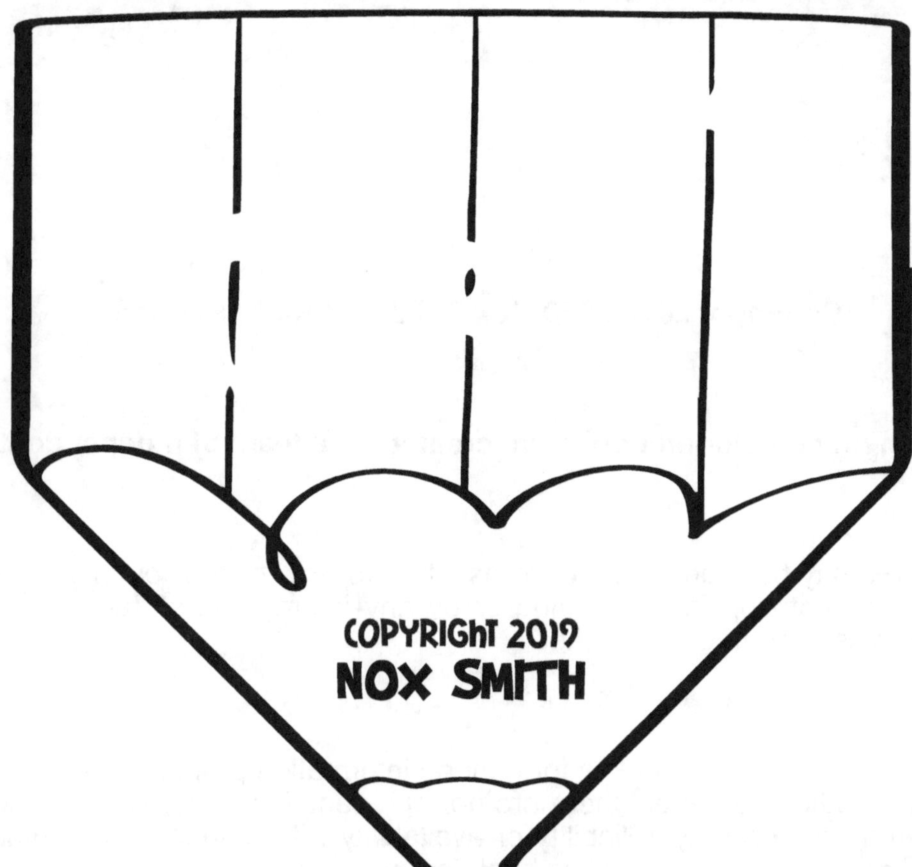

ANIMAL
COLOR BY NUMBER
FOR ADULTS
COPYRIGHT 2019
NOX SMITH

Copyright 2018-2019 Nox Smith. All Right Reserved.

Nox Smith brand coloring books are created by a team of independent artists.

No part of this book may be reproduced or transmitted in any form or by any means, electronic or mechanical,including photocopying, recording or by any information storage and retrieval system, without written permission form the publisher.

The information provided with this book is for general information purpose only. While we try to keep the information up-to-date and correct there are no representation or warranties, express or implied, about the completeness, accuracy, reliability or availability with respect to the information, product, service, or related graphics contained in this book for any purpose.

THIS BOOK
BELONG TO

COLOR PALETTE

(0) White

(1) Yellow

(2) Light Orange

(3) Dark Orange

(4) Cream

(5) Red

(6) Dark Red

(7) Pink

(8) Violet

(9) Dark Pink

(10) Dark Purple

(11) Light Blue

(12) Sky Blue

(13) Medium Blue

(14) Dark Blue

(15) Yellow Green

(16) Medium Green

(17) Bright Green

(18) Dark Green

(19) Tan

(20) Light Brown

(21) Dark Brown

(22) Light Gray

(23) Dark Gray

(24) Black

The world is my canvas and I create my reality.

COLOR PALETTE

0	White	12	Sky Blue
1	Yellow	13	Medium Blue
2	Light Orange	14	Dark Blue
3	Dark Orange	15	Yellow Green
4	Cream	16	Medium Green
5	Red	17	Bright Green
6	Dark Red	18	Dark Green
7	Pink	19	Tan
8	Violet	20	Light Brown
9	Dark Pink	21	Dark Brown
10	Dark Purple	22	Light Gray
11	Light Blue	23	Dark Gray
		24	Black

The world is my canvas and I create my reality.

COLOR PALETTE

- (0) White
- (1) Yellow
- (2) Light Orange
- (3) Dark Orange
- (4) Cream
- (5) Red
- (6) Dark Red
- (7) Pink
- (8) Violet
- (9) Dark Pink
- (10) Dark Purple
- (11) Light Blue
- (12) Sky Blue
- (13) Medium Blue
- (14) Dark Blue
- (15) Yellow Green
- (16) Medium Green
- (17) Bright Green
- (18) Dark Green
- (19) Tan
- (20) Light Brown
- (21) Dark Brown
- (22) Light Gray
- (23) Dark Gray
- (24) Black

The world is my canvas and I create my reality.

COLOR PALETTE

Number	Color		Number	Color
0	White		12	Sky Blue
1	Yellow		13	Medium Blue
2	Light Orange		14	Dark Blue
3	Dark Orange		15	Yellow Green
4	Cream		16	Medium Green
5	Red		17	Bright Green
6	Dark Red		18	Dark Green
7	Pink		19	Tan
8	Violet		20	Light Brown
9	Dark Pink		21	Dark Brown
10	Dark Purple		22	Light Gray
11	Light Blue		23	Dark Gray
			24	Black

The world is my canvas and I create my reality.

COLOR PALETTE

0. White
1. Yellow
2. Light Orange
3. Dark Orange
4. Cream
5. Red
6. Dark Red
7. Pink
8. Violet
9. Dark Pink
10. Dark Purple
11. Light Blue
12. Sky Blue
13. Medium Blue
14. Dark Blue
15. Yellow Green
16. Medium Green
17. Bright Green
18. Dark Green
19. Tan
20. Light Brown
21. Dark Brown
22. Light Gray
23. Dark Gray
24. Black

The world is my canvas and I create my reality.

COLOR PALETTE

0 White
1 Yellow
2 Light Orange
3 Dark Orange
4 Cream
5 Red
6 Dark Red
7 Pink
8 Violet
9 Dark Pink
10 Dark Purple
11 Light Blue

12 Sky Blue
13 Medium Blue
14 Dark Blue
15 Yellow Green
16 Medium Green
17 Bright Green
18 Dark Green
19 Tan
20 Light Brown
21 Dark Brown
22 Light Gray
23 Dark Gray
24 Black

The world is my canvas and I create my reality.

COLOR PALETTE

(0) White	(12) Sky Blue
(1) Yellow	(13) Medium Blue
(2) Light Orange	(14) Dark Blue
(3) Dark Orange	(15) Yellow Green
(4) Cream	(16) Medium Green
(5) Red	(17) Bright Green
(6) Dark Red	(18) Dark Green
(7) Pink	(19) Tan
(8) Violet	(20) Light Brown
(9) Dark Pink	(21) Dark Brown
(10) Dark Purple	(22) Light Gray
(11) Light Blue	(23) Dark Gray
	(24) Black

The world is my canvas and I create my reality.

COLOR PALETTE

(0) White	(12) Sky Blue
(1) Yellow	(13) Medium Blue
(2) Light Orange	(14) Dark Blue
(3) Dark Orange	(15) Yellow Green
(4) Cream	(16) Medium Green
(5) Red	(17) Bright Green
(6) Dark Red	(18) Dark Green
(7) Pink	(19) Tan
(8) Violet	(20) Light Brown
(9) Dark Pink	(21) Dark Brown
(10) Dark Purple	(22) Light Gray
(11) Light Blue	(23) Dark Gray
	(24) Black

The world is my canvas and I create my reality.

COLOR PALETTE

- (0) White
- (1) Yellow
- (2) Light Orange
- (3) Dark Orange
- (4) Cream
- (5) Red
- (6) Dark Red
- (7) Pink
- (8) Violet
- (9) Dark Pink
- (10) Dark Purple
- (11) Light Blue
- (12) Sky Blue
- (13) Medium Blue
- (14) Dark Blue
- (15) Yellow Green
- (16) Medium Green
- (17) Bright Green
- (18) Dark Green
- (19) Tan
- (20) Light Brown
- (21) Dark Brown
- (22) Light Gray
- (23) Dark Gray
- (24) Black

The world is my canvas and I create my reality.

COLOR PALETTE

(0) White	(12) Sky Blue
(1) Yellow	(13) Medium Blue
(2) Light Orange	(14) Dark Blue
(3) Dark Orange	(15) Yellow Green
(4) Cream	(16) Medium Green
(5) Red	(17) Bright Green
(6) Dark Red	(18) Dark Green
(7) Pink	(19) Tan
(8) Violet	(20) Light Brown
(9) Dark Pink	(21) Dark Brown
(10) Dark Purple	(22) Light Gray
(11) Light Blue	(23) Dark Gray
	(24) Black

The world is my canvas and I create my reality.

COLOR PALETTE

(0) White	(12) Sky Blue
(1) Yellow	(13) Medium Blue
(2) Light Orange	(14) Dark Blue
(3) Dark Orange	(15) Yellow Green
(4) Cream	(16) Medium Green
(5) Red	(17) Bright Green
(6) Dark Red	(18) Dark Green
(7) Pink	(19) Tan
(8) Violet	(20) Light Brown
(9) Dark Pink	(21) Dark Brown
(10) Dark Purple	(22) Light Gray
(11) Light Blue	(23) Dark Gray
	(24) Black

The world is my canvas and I create my reality.

COLOR PALETTE

0 White	12 Sky Blue
1 Yellow	13 Medium Blue
2 Light Orange	14 Dark Blue
3 Dark Orange	15 Yellow Green
4 Cream	16 Medium Green
5 Red	17 Bright Green
6 Dark Red	18 Dark Green
7 Pink	19 Tan
8 Violet	20 Light Brown
9 Dark Pink	21 Dark Brown
10 Dark Purple	22 Light Gray
11 Light Blue	23 Dark Gray
	24 Black

The world is my canvas and I create my reality.

COLOR PALETTE

- (0) White
- (1) Yellow
- (2) Light Orange
- (3) Dark Orange
- (4) Cream
- (5) Red
- (6) Dark Red
- (7) Pink
- (8) Violet
- (9) Dark Pink
- (10) Dark Purple
- (11) Light Blue
- (12) Sky Blue
- (13) Medium Blue
- (14) Dark Blue
- (15) Yellow Green
- (16) Medium Green
- (17) Bright Green
- (18) Dark Green
- (19) Tan
- (20) Light Brown
- (21) Dark Brown
- (22) Light Gray
- (23) Dark Gray
- (24) Black

The world is my canvas and I create my reality.

COLOR PALETTE

(0) White	(12) Sky Blue
(1) Yellow	(13) Medium Blue
(2) Light Orange	(14) Dark Blue
(3) Dark Orange	(15) Yellow Green
(4) Cream	(16) Medium Green
(5) Red	(17) Bright Green
(6) Dark Red	(18) Dark Green
(7) Pink	(19) Tan
(8) Violet	(20) Light Brown
(9) Dark Pink	(21) Dark Brown
(10) Dark Purple	(22) Light Gray
(11) Light Blue	(23) Dark Gray
	(24) Black

The world is my canvas and I create my reality.

COLOR PALETTE

Code	Color	Code	Color
(0)	White	(12)	Sky Blue
(1)	Yellow	(13)	Medium Blue
(2)	Light Orange	(14)	Dark Blue
(3)	Dark Orange	(15)	Yellow Green
(4)	Cream	(16)	Medium Green
(5)	Red	(17)	Bright Green
(6)	Dark Red	(18)	Dark Green
(7)	Pink	(19)	Tan
(8)	Violet	(20)	Light Brown
(9)	Dark Pink	(21)	Dark Brown
(10)	Dark Purple	(22)	Light Gray
(11)	Light Blue	(23)	Dark Gray
		(24)	Black

The world is my canvas and I create my reality.

COLOR PALETTE

<table>
<tr><td>

- (0) White
- (1) Yellow
- (2) Light Orange
- (3) Dark Orange
- (4) Cream
- (5) Red
- (6) Dark Red
- (7) Pink
- (8) Violet
- (9) Dark Pink
- (10) Dark Purple
- (11) Light Blue

</td><td>

- (12) Sky Blue
- (13) Medium Blue
- (14) Dark Blue
- (15) Yellow Green
- (16) Medium Green
- (17) Bright Green
- (18) Dark Green
- (19) Tan
- (20) Light Brown
- (21) Dark Brown
- (22) Light Gray
- (23) Dark Gray
- (24) Black

</td></tr>
</table>

The world is my canvas and I create my reality.

COLOR PALETTE

- ⓪ White
- ① Yellow
- ② Light Orange
- ③ Dark Orange
- ④ Cream
- ⑤ Red
- ⑥ Dark Red
- ⑦ Pink
- ⑧ Violet
- ⑨ Dark Pink
- ⑩ Dark Purple
- ⑪ Light Blue
- ⑫ Sky Blue
- ⑬ Medium Blue
- ⑭ Dark Blue
- ⑮ Yellow Green
- ⑯ Medium Green
- ⑰ Bright Green
- ⑱ Dark Green
- ⑲ Tan
- ⑳ Light Brown
- ㉑ Dark Brown
- ㉒ Light Gray
- ㉓ Dark Gray
- ㉔ Black

The world is my canvas and I create my reality.

COLOR PALETTE

0	White	12	Sky Blue
1	Yellow	13	Medium Blue
2	Light Orange	14	Dark Blue
3	Dark Orange	15	Yellow Green
4	Cream	16	Medium Green
5	Red	17	Bright Green
6	Dark Red	18	Dark Green
7	Pink	19	Tan
8	Violet	20	Light Brown
9	Dark Pink	21	Dark Brown
10	Dark Purple	22	Light Gray
11	Light Blue	23	Dark Gray
		24	Black

The world is my canvas and I create my reality.

COLOR PALETTE

- ⓪ White
- ① Yellow
- ② Light Orange
- ③ Dark Orange
- ④ Cream
- ⑤ Red
- ⑥ Dark Red
- ⑦ Pink
- ⑧ Violet
- ⑨ Dark Pink
- ⑩ Dark Purple
- ⑪ Light Blue
- ⑫ Sky Blue
- ⑬ Medium Blue
- ⑭ Dark Blue
- ⑮ Yellow Green
- ⑯ Medium Green
- ⑰ Bright Green
- ⑱ Dark Green
- ⑲ Tan
- ⑳ Light Brown
- ㉑ Dark Brown
- ㉒ Light Gray
- ㉓ Dark Gray
- ㉔ Black

The world is my canvas and I create my reality.

COLOR PALETTE

(0) White	(12) Sky Blue
(1) Yellow	(13) Medium Blue
(2) Light Orange	(14) Dark Blue
(3) Dark Orange	(15) Yellow Green
(4) Cream	(16) Medium Green
(5) Red	(17) Bright Green
(6) Dark Red	(18) Dark Green
(7) Pink	(19) Tan
(8) Violet	(20) Light Brown
(9) Dark Pink	(21) Dark Brown
(10) Dark Purple	(22) Light Gray
(11) Light Blue	(23) Dark Gray
	(24) Black

The world is my canvas and I create my reality.

COLOR PALETTE

- (0) White
- (1) Yellow
- (2) Light Orange
- (3) Dark Orange
- (4) Cream
- (5) Red
- (6) Dark Red
- (7) Pink
- (8) Violet
- (9) Dark Pink
- (10) Dark Purple
- (11) Light Blue
- (12) Sky Blue
- (13) Medium Blue
- (14) Dark Blue
- (15) Yellow Green
- (16) Medium Green
- (17) Bright Green
- (18) Dark Green
- (19) Tan
- (20) Light Brown
- (21) Dark Brown
- (22) Light Gray
- (23) Dark Gray
- (24) Black

The world is my canvas and I create my reality.

COLOR PALETTE

(0)	White	(12)	Sky Blue
(1)	Yellow	(13)	Medium Blue
(2)	Light Orange	(14)	Dark Blue
(3)	Dark Orange	(15)	Yellow Green
(4)	Cream	(16)	Medium Green
(5)	Red	(17)	Bright Green
(6)	Dark Red	(18)	Dark Green
(7)	Pink	(19)	Tan
(8)	Violet	(20)	Light Brown
(9)	Dark Pink	(21)	Dark Brown
(10)	Dark Purple	(22)	Light Gray
(11)	Light Blue	(23)	Dark Gray
		(24)	Black

The world is my canvas and I create my reality.

COLOR PALETTE

- (0) White
- (1) Yellow
- (2) Light Orange
- (3) Dark Orange
- (4) Cream
- (5) Red
- (6) Dark Red
- (7) Pink
- (8) Violet
- (9) Dark Pink
- (10) Dark Purple
- (11) Light Blue
- (12) Sky Blue
- (13) Medium Blue
- (14) Dark Blue
- (15) Yellow Green
- (16) Medium Green
- (17) Bright Green
- (18) Dark Green
- (19) Tan
- (20) Light Brown
- (21) Dark Brown
- (22) Light Gray
- (23) Dark Gray
- (24) Black

The world is my canvas and I create my reality.

COLOR PALETTE

- (0) White
- (1) Yellow
- (2) Light Orange
- (3) Dark Orange
- (4) Cream
- (5) Red
- (6) Dark Red
- (7) Pink
- (8) Violet
- (9) Dark Pink
- (10) Dark Purple
- (11) Light Blue
- (12) Sky Blue
- (13) Medium Blue
- (14) Dark Blue
- (15) Yellow Green
- (16) Medium Green
- (17) Bright Green
- (18) Dark Green
- (19) Tan
- (20) Light Brown
- (21) Dark Brown
- (22) Light Gray
- (23) Dark Gray
- (24) Black

The world is my canvas and I create my reality.

COLOR PALETTE

(0) White	(12) Sky Blue
(1) Yellow	(13) Medium Blue
(2) Light Orange	(14) Dark Blue
(3) Dark Orange	(15) Yellow Green
(4) Cream	(16) Medium Green
(5) Red	(17) Bright Green
(6) Dark Red	(18) Dark Green
(7) Pink	(19) Tan
(8) Violet	(20) Light Brown
(9) Dark Pink	(21) Dark Brown
(10) Dark Purple	(22) Light Gray
(11) Light Blue	(23) Dark Gray
	(24) Black

The world is my canvas and I create my reality.

COLOR PALETTE

- (0) White
- (1) Yellow
- (2) Light Orange
- (3) Dark Orange
- (4) Cream
- (5) Red
- (6) Dark Red
- (7) Pink
- (8) Violet
- (9) Dark Pink
- (10) Dark Purple
- (11) Light Blue
- (12) Sky Blue
- (13) Medium Blue
- (14) Dark Blue
- (15) Yellow Green
- (16) Medium Green
- (17) Bright Green
- (18) Dark Green
- (19) Tan
- (20) Light Brown
- (21) Dark Brown
- (22) Light Gray
- (23) Dark Gray
- (24) Black

The world is my canvas and I create my reality.

COLOR PALETTE

(0) White
(1) Yellow
(2) Light Orange
(3) Dark Orange
(4) Cream
(5) Red
(6) Dark Red
(7) Pink
(8) Violet
(9) Dark Pink
(10) Dark Purple
(11) Light Blue

(12) Sky Blue
(13) Medium Blue
(14) Dark Blue
(15) Yellow Green
(16) Medium Green
(17) Bright Green
(18) Dark Green
(19) Tan
(20) Light Brown
(21) Dark Brown
(22) Light Gray
(23) Dark Gray
(24) Black

The world is my canvas and I create my reality.

COLOR PALETTE

#	Color	#	Color
0	White	12	Sky Blue
1	Yellow	13	Medium Blue
2	Light Orange	14	Dark Blue
3	Dark Orange	15	Yellow Green
4	Cream	16	Medium Green
5	Red	17	Bright Green
6	Dark Red	18	Dark Green
7	Pink	19	Tan
8	Violet	20	Light Brown
9	Dark Pink	21	Dark Brown
10	Dark Purple	22	Light Gray
11	Light Blue	23	Dark Gray
		24	Black

The world is my canvas and I create my reality.

www.ingramcontent.com/pod-product-compliance
Lightning Source LLC
Chambersburg PA
CBHW081455250726
48662CB00009B/3100